Pebble® Plus

Life around the World

Birthdays in Many Cultures

by Martha E. H. Rustad

Consulting Editor: Gail Saunders-Smith, PhD

Capstone press®

Mankato, Minnesota

Pebble Plus is published by Capstone Press,
151 Good Counsel Drive, P.O. Box 669, Mankato, Minnesota 56002.
www.capstonepress.com

1 2 3 4 5 6 13 12 11 10 09 08

Library of Congress Cataloging-in-Publication Data
Rustad, Martha E. H. (Martha Elizabeth Hillman), 1975–
    Birthdays in many cultures / by Martha E. H. Rustad.
    p. cm. — (Pebble plus. Life around the world)
    Summary: "Simple text and photographs present birthdays in many cultures" — Provided by publisher.
    Includes bibliographical references and index.
    ISBN-13: 978-1-4296-1741-3 (hardcover)
    ISBN-10: 1-4296-1741-1 (hardcover)
    1. Birthdays — Juvenile literature. I. Title. II. Series.
GT2430.R87 2009
394.2 — dc22   2008003340

Editorial Credits
Sarah L. Schuette, editor; Kim Brown, book designer; Alison Thiele, set designer; Wanda Winch, photo researcher

Photo Credits
Alamy/David Hancock, 5; Keith Dannemiller, 7; View Stock China, 21
Art Life Images Inc./Helena Bergengren, 11
Capstone Press/Karon Dubke, cover, 1
Getty Images Inc./LOOK/Sabine Duerichen, 9; Taxi/Edgardo Contreras, 19
The Image Works/Julia Cumes, 13; VISUM/George Schoenharting, 17
Peter Arnold/Nigel Dickinson, 15

Note to Parents and Teachers

The Life around the World set supports national social studies standards related to
culture and geography. This book describes and illustrates birthdays in many cultures.
The images support early readers in understanding the text. The repetition of words and
phrases helps early readers learn new words. This book also introduces early readers
to subject-specific vocabulary words, which are defined in the Glossary section. Early
readers may need assistance to read some words and to use the Table of Contents,
Glossary, Read More, Internet Sites, and Index sections of the book.

Table of Contents

Birthday Parties

People celebrate
their birthdays
in many cultures.

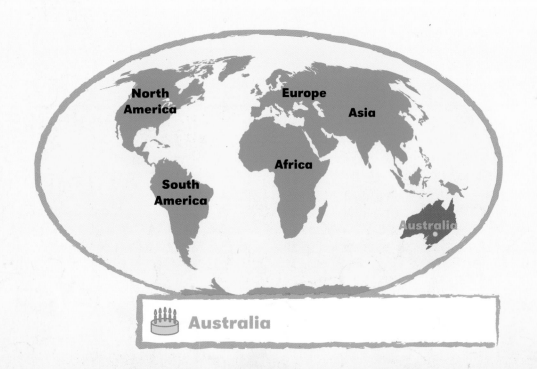

Australia

People play games
on their birthdays.
A girl in Mexico
breaks open a piñata.

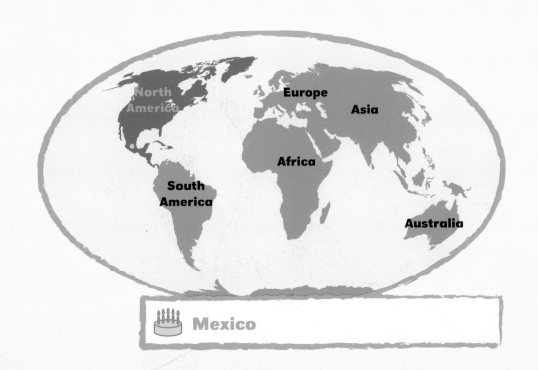

North America

Europe

Asia

Africa

South America

Australia

Mexico

A boy in the United States
bobs for apples
at his birthday party.

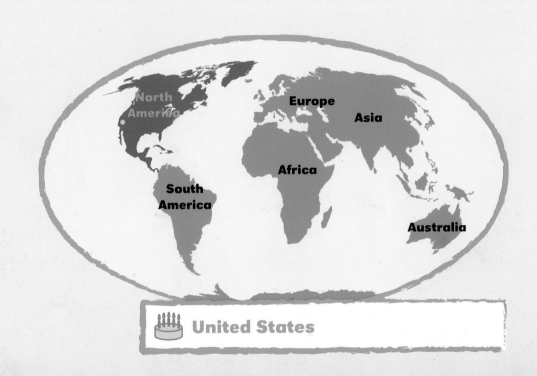

North America

Europe

Asia

Africa

South America

Australia

United States

A boy in Sweden
has breakfast in bed
to celebrate his birthday.

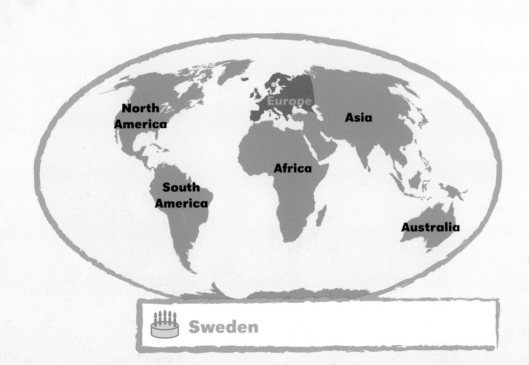

Sweden

More Birthday Fun

A boy in South Africa
blows out candles
on his birthday cake.

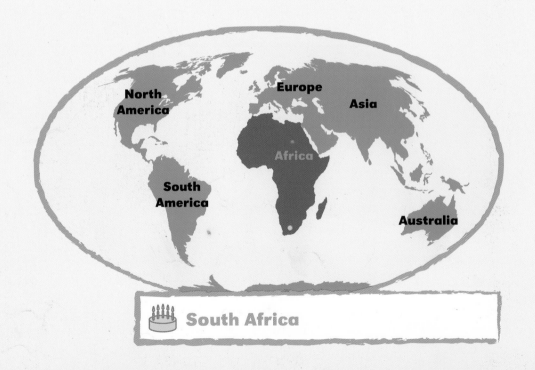

North America · Europe · Asia · Africa · South America · Australia

South Africa

A boy in England
goes shopping
on his birthday.

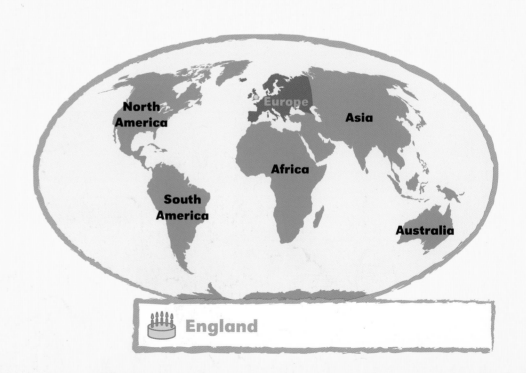

England

A boy in Germany

eats at a restaurant

on his birthday.

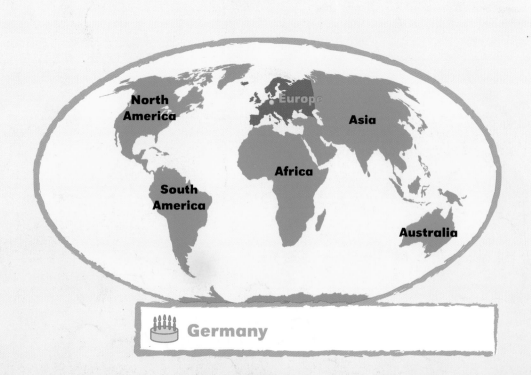

North
America

Europe

Asia

Africa

South
America

Australia

Germany

People open gifts
on their birthdays.
A girl in Mexico picks
which gift to open first.

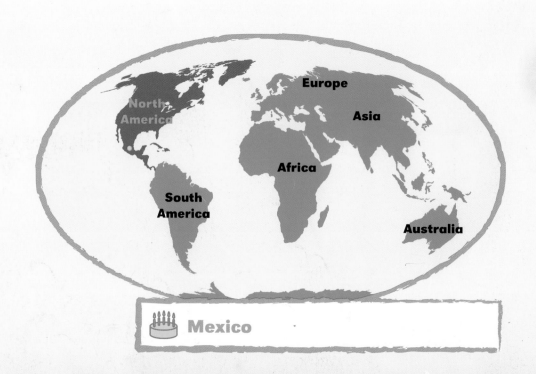

Mexico

Your Birthday

Around the world,
people laugh and play
on their birthdays.
When is your birthday?

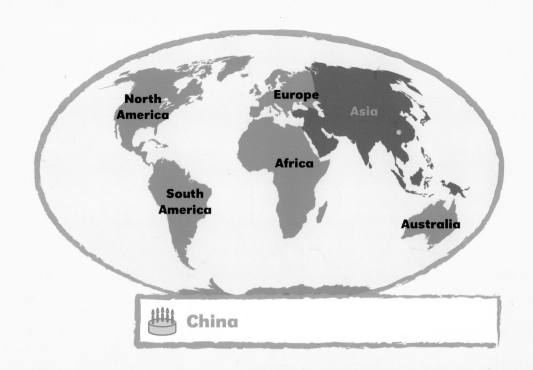

North
America

Europe

Asia

Africa

South
America

Australia

China

Glossary

celebrate — to do something fun, like having a party

culture — the way of life, ideas, customs, and traditions of a group of people

piñata — a container filled with candies and gifts; piñatas are popular at Latin American parties and celebrations.

restaurant — a place where people pay to eat meals

Read More

Powell, Jillian. *A Birthday.* Why Is This Day Special? North Mankato, Minn.: Smart Apple Media, 2007.

Schaefer, Ted. *When Is Your Birthday?* Science about Me. Vero Beach, Fla.: Rourke, 2007.

Stewart, Amber. *Birthday Countdown.* Columbus, Ohio: Gingham Dog Press, 2007.

Internet Sites

FactHound offers a safe, fun way to find Internet sites related to this book. All of the sites on FactHound have been researched by our staff.

Here's how:

1. Visit *www.facthound.com*

2. Choose your grade level.

3. Type in this book ID **1429617411** for age-appropriate sites. You may also browse subjects by clicking on letters, or by clicking on pictures and words.

4. Click on the **Fetch It** button.

FactHound will fetch the best sites for you!

Index

Word Count: 108
Grade: 1
Early-Intervention Level: 18